ANTS FOR KIDS

ANTS FOR KIDS

A JUNIOR SCIENTIST'S GUIDE
to Queens, Drones, and the Hidden World of Ants

JUNIOR SCIENTISTS

BEVERLY GERDEMAN, PhD

ROCKRIDGE PRESS

To my Junior Scientists: Ana, Erika, Mauria, and Diedre!

For general information on our other products and services or to obtain technical support, please contact our Customer Care Department within the United States at (866) 744-2665, or outside the United States at (510) 253-0500.

Rockridge Press publishes its books in a variety of electronic and print formats. Some content that appears in print may not be available in electronic books, and vice versa.

Interior and Designer: John Calmeyer
Art Producer: Janice Ackerman
Editor: Mary Colgan
Production Editor: Rachel Taenzler

Cover Photography: ©Yusnizam Yusof/Shutterstock Illustrations: ©2020 Kate Francis. Interior Photography: ii: ©Dwi Yulianto/shutterstock; iv: ©Antagain/istock; vi: ©Yusnizam Yusof/shutterstock; viii–p. 1: ©Chik_77/shutterstock; p. 2: Courtesy of Simon Fraser University Public Affairs and Media Relations; pp. 5–6: ©Alex Wild; p. 10: ©Alex Wild; p. 13: ©Alex Wild; p. 14: ©Cabezonication/istock; p. 16: ©Redmond Durrell/Alamy Stock Photo; p. 19 top: ©Redmond Durrell/Alamy Stock Photo; p. 19 bottom: ©spxChrome/istock; p. 21: ©Alex Wild; p. 22: ©Oliver Thompson-Holmes/Alamy Stock Photo; p. 24: ©Alex Wild; p. 25 top: ©Redmond Durrell/Alamy Stock Photo; p. 25 bottom: ©spxChrome/istock; p. 27: ©Alex Wild; p. 32: ©Redmond Durrell/Alamy Stock Photo; p. 34–37: ©Redmond Durrell/Alamy Stock Photo; pp. 38–39: ©Adisak Mitrprayoon/istock; pp. 40–55: ©Alex Wild; p. 56: ©Pavel Krasensky/Shutterstock

ISBN: Print 978-1-64876-019-8
eBook 978-1-64876-020-4
R0

Printed in China

CONTENTS

WELCOME, JUNIOR SCIENTIST!

Have you ever watched ants and wanted to know more about them? Perhaps you've seen hundreds of ants scurrying in a long line and questioned where they were going. Do you wonder what their homes are like, or why some ants can fly? If these are things you've thought about, you are a junior scientist!

In this book, you will learn about these amazing insects—where they live, how they communicate, and what they eat. You will learn about ant **colonies** and the roles of different family members—queens, **drones**, and workers. Finally, you will get up close and personal with some of the most amazing ant **species** in the world along with common ants you may see in your own backyard.

Do you want to observe ants firsthand? Great! This book will show you how. It also has tips on starting your own ant farm so you can spy on the secret lives of ants. Everything you ever wanted to know about ants is right at your fingertips. Let's start exploring!

PART ONE

AMAZING ANTS

Ants are everywhere—almost. Antarctica, Greenland, and Iceland are the only regions that are currently ant-free. However, ants are on the move and populating new areas. Ants are so small that they can easily stow away in cargo ships, airplanes, and even backpacks! Scientists who study ants are called **myrmecologists**. They think Earth is home to 10 quadrillion (16 zeros!) of these tiny insects, but no one really knows for sure. More than 15,000 species have been identified so far, but many scientists think there could be at least 9,000 more.

Ants of the Past

Ants are ancient. We have **fossils** to prove it! Some ants were fossilized when they got trapped in tree sap that hardened into amber. Others got stuck in mud and left imprints that turned to stone. *Titanomyrma lubei*, the giant hummingbird-size ant from Wyoming, was fossilized this way. The oldest ant fossils are 100 million years old. This is about when flower and fruit plants started to grow on Earth. Scientists now know that ants have been around much longer. Modern tests on ants' cells prove that they appeared 140 to 168 million years ago.

Sixty-six million years ago, there was a global event that caused the death of most animals. Most scientists believe an asteroid hit Earth. Dinosaurs and 80 percent of the world's species were wiped out, but ants survived. Like today's ants, ancient ants were **omnivores** and ate everything from dead animals to nectar, seeds, and fruit. With so many foods to choose from, ants were able to survive in new habitats. As the continents moved apart, ants eventually spread to all parts of the globe. They evolved, or gradually changed, into the many species on Earth today.

The prehistoric ant *Titanomyrma lubei* was two inches long, about as big as a modern hummingbird.

DID YOU KNOW?

The smallest ant in the world so far is *Carebara atoma*. It is about as big as a poppy seed. The largest is *Dinoponera gigantea*—about as long as a silver dollar is wide.

Ants: Antennae to Feet

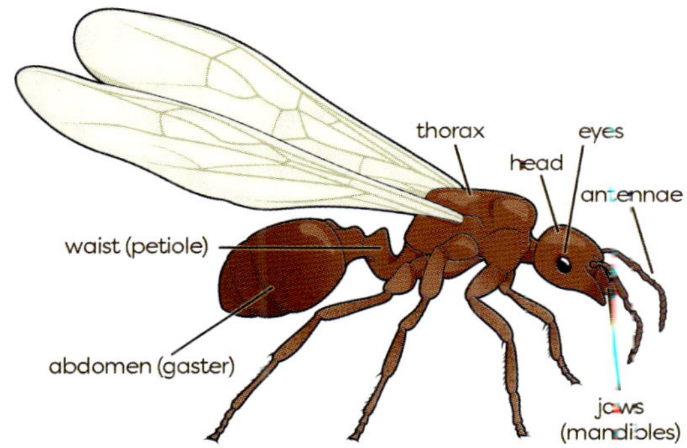

Ants are insects—**invertebrates** with no bones and a tough outer shell called an exoskeleton. Like all insects, ants have three body parts: a head, thorax, and abdomen. Not all ants have eyes (really!), but if they do, they are on the head. Ants have two large eyes, called **compound eyes**, and three little eyes, called **ocelli**, located on their heads. They have two bent antennae and jaws, called mandibles. The mandibles can be different shapes depending on an ant's job—fighting, digging, or carrying prey.

The thorax is where an ant's six legs and two pairs of wings (if the ant has them) are attached. Ants have a very skinny waist, called a **petiole**, and a large rounded abdomen. The plump part of the abdomen is called a **gaster**. It holds all the ant's guts. Each ant's waxy exoskeleton has a scent. The scent is the same for ants from the same colony, so they can recognize one another by smell. Ants may be small, but they are super strong. They can lift 50 times their weight. That's like a 50-pound kid lifting a small car!

DID YOU KNOW?

Termites are insects that are often confused with ants. Both insects are small, live in colonies, and build nests, but they are not related. Termite wings are the same size, while ant forewings are bigger than their hindwings. Termites also don't have skinny waists like ants do.

An Ant's Life

Each ant begins life as a tiny oval egg in the dark nursery chamber of the nest. The queen decides if an egg will be a worker or drone when she lays it. In most species, a fertilized egg will become a worker or a queen. Unfertilized eggs become drones. You will learn more about each type of ant later.

Some worker ants are nurse ants, which means it is their job to take care of the eggs. They lick the eggs to remove bacteria or fungi, which keeps the eggs healthy. After one or two weeks, the eggs hatch into baby ants called larvae. They don't have legs or eyes and look a little like white squash with crooked necks. The larvae have spines that protect them. The spines also help them stick together, like Velcro, so nurse ants can quickly grab large bundles of larvae and escape to

Nurse ant caring for larvae

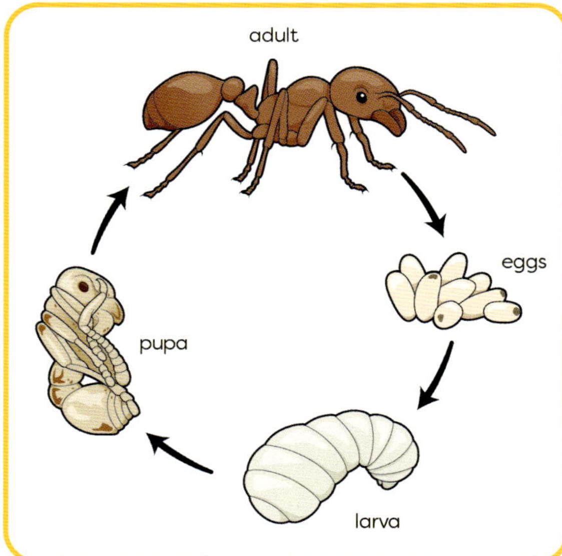

Life cycle of an ant

safety if they are in danger. The larvae's job is to eat the food the workers bring and to grow.

About a month later, larvae of some species spin cocoons and become **pupae**. They are placed in a dry chamber in the ant nest. Nurse ants constantly move the pupae around the nest to make sure the temperature and humidity, or amount of moisture in the air, are just right for them. When it's time for the adults to emerge from the pupae, workers tear open the cocoons to free them. Every year, ants produce a new generation, or group, of offspring.

DID YOU KNOW?

There are about 15 species of exploding ants. *Colobopsis explodens* is an ant that lives in Southeast Asia. If threatened, it can squeeze its body so hard that it blows itself up, spattering a sticky yellow gunk that can kill or stop its enemies.

Ants with a pupa

Ant Colonies

Ants are social insects, which means they live together and work as a team. Ant communities are called colonies. Depending on the species, an ant colony can have hundreds or even millions of ants. Every one of those ants has a role—either queen, drone, or worker. Everything each ant does is for the good of the entire colony.

In many ways, a colony works like one giant organism. This is called **eusociality**. Eusocial insects like bees, wasps, and ants, are very successful.

Let's meet the members of an ant colony. We'll start with a very special ant—the queen!

DID YOU KNOW?

Pliny and Herodotus, ancient Greek historians, told a legend of gold-mining ants. It was based on the ants' habit of collecting small pebbles to lay on their anthills. The author of this book actually found tiny gold nuggets while studying an ant nest in the Pacific. Are gold-mining ants legend or truth?

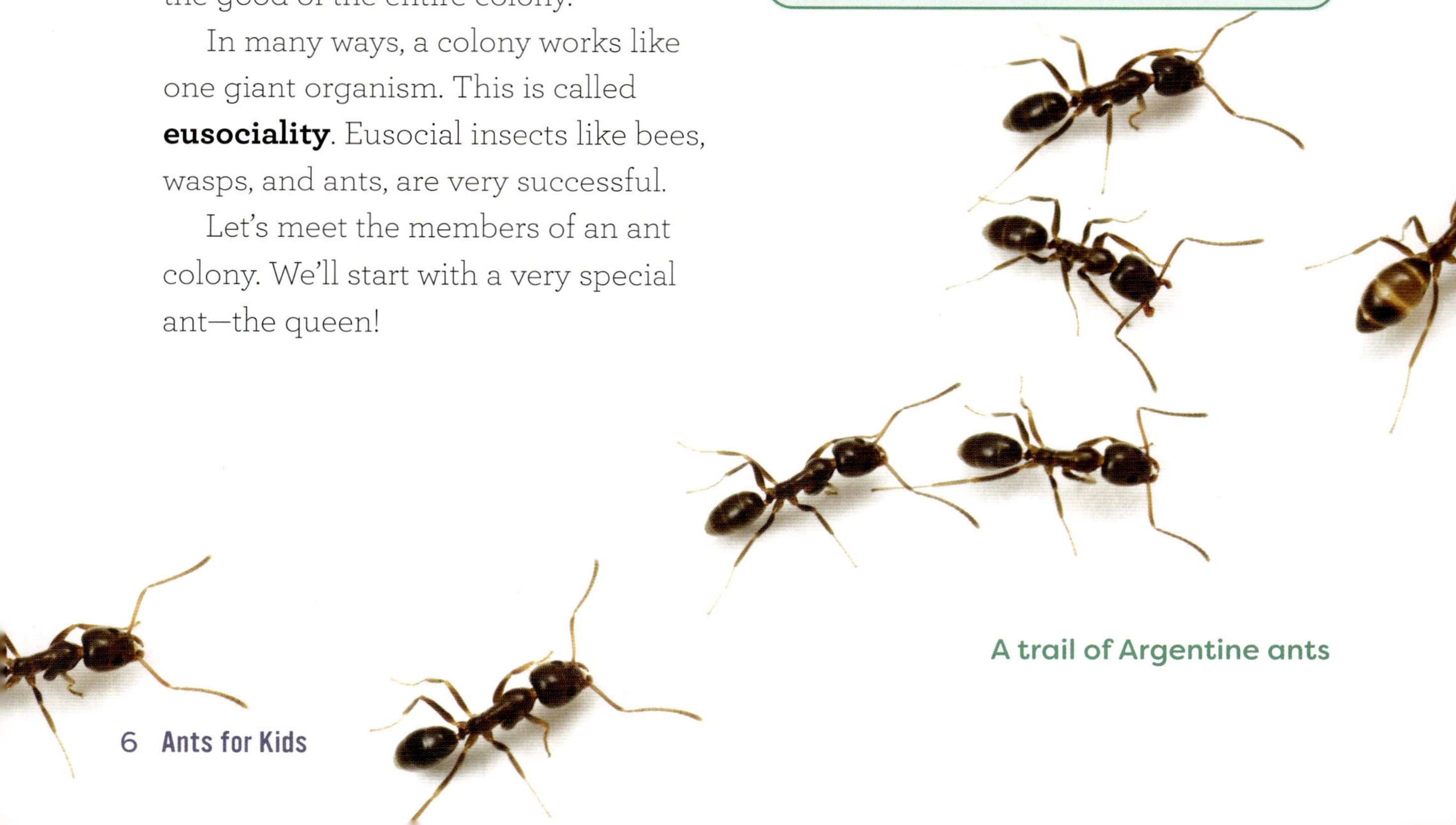

A trail of Argentine ants

QUEENS

The queen is powerful. She is responsible for laying all the eggs in the colony—sometimes thousands a day for her entire life. She is the one who decides if an egg will become a worker or a drone. She makes this decision depending on what the colony needs. She can also make more queens. Any fertilized egg can become a queen if the larva is fed lots of nutritious food when it hatches.

When a new queen comes out of a pupa, she is already larger than the workers and usually has wings. Queens can live 5 to 6 years in nature, but with luck and good care, they can live up to 30 years! If a queen dies, the colony usually dies, too.

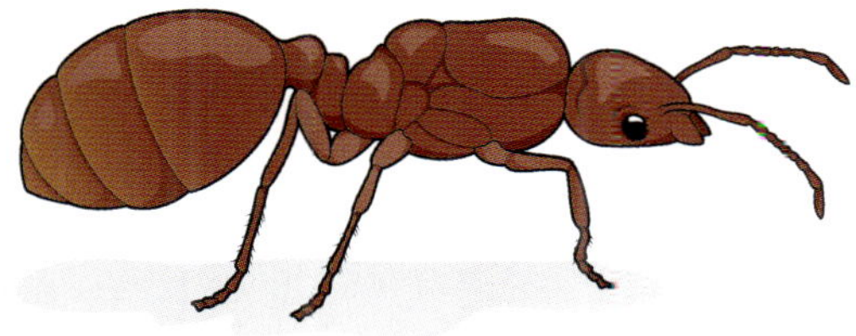

Queen ant

DID YOU KNOW?

Some ant colonies have more than one queen. If all the colonies in one area become interconnected, a supercolony is formed! The largest supercolony in the world is 3,700 miles long and has billions of ants.

DRONES

Male ants are called drones. They begin life as unfertilized eggs. Drones have wings and are smaller than their worker sisters. They look more like small wasps than ants. While all the other ants in the colony have stingers, drones don't. Also unlike their sisters, drones don't have any chores to do in the colony. They spend most of their time cleaning themselves or waiting to be fed by workers. Drones have one very important purpose—to mate with queens. Once they do that, they die. Most drones have short lives.

Drone ant

WORKERS

Worker ant

Ant colonies are like factories churning out workers and drones. Most of the ants in a colony are workers, which are all female. Workers begin their lives as fertilized eggs. Eggs of workers look no different from the eggs of drones or future queens. When the eggs hatch, nurse workers feed the larvae liquids. Some species feed their larvae small pieces of insects or seeds. Worker larvae may seem helpless, but the larvae of some species help feed the adults by chewing solid food and turning it into liquids. Once a worker becomes an adult, she begins a selfless life of work for the good of the colony.

Not all workers in the colony are equal. Older workers are not valued as much as younger workers and perform riskier jobs than when they were young. Young ants care for the larvae inside the nest where it is safe. They have a higher status than the older ants that risk their lives looking for food or defending the nest.

Some ant species have two types of workers: majors and minors. Major workers have large heads with big mandibles. They work as soldiers to defend the nest. They have a higher status than minor workers, which are regular-size.

An ant's odor may be associated with its job. Leafcutter ant workers that carry trash or dead ants out of the nest smell like rot and death. They may have diseases that could kill the entire colony. Other workers stay away from them to keep the colony healthy and safe.

Carpenter ant major workers (right) can be twice as large as minor workers (left).

Inside the colony, new workers care for the eggs and larvae. Some clean the pupae and help them come out of their cocoons. Others clean and feed the queen. Some workers have jobs outside the nest. They might defend the nest entrance or protect a food source. They also may look for food or build new tunnels. Outside jobs are risky, so they are given to the older workers with lower status. Workers can live for several years and can even remember things and learn from experience.

DID YOU KNOW?

Leafcutter ants farm fungus—which makes a lot of waste. This smelly waste is dumped outside the colony in piles. The ants are so grossed out by its smell that human farmers spread it around their crops to protect plants from leafcutter ants!

A drone (left), queen (right), and worker (bottom) carpenter ant

Building a Home

Queen ants begin digging the first chamber of the nest shortly after mating.

So, how does an ant colony start? Ants swarm during warm weather. This is when new queens and drones fly from the nest in large groups to mate. Only the strongest will survive to make new colonies. Once a queen mates, she snaps off her wings, digs a small chamber in the ground using her mandibles and front legs, and lays her first eggs. She cleans and cares for them until a few workers hatch to take over nursery duty. As more workers hatch, they divide the chores so the queen can concentrate on just laying eggs. A new colony is born!

The workers continue digging tunnels and chambers, or rooms, to make space for their rapidly growing family. The chambers may have low or high ceilings and smooth floors. Neat tunnels connect all the chambers together. Workers are tidy. They keep the nest clean by carrying garbage and poop far away to trash chambers at its edge, called **middens**. Some chambers are used only for raising the young. Others are pantries full of stored food. The queen ant has her very own egg-laying chamber. As the nest grows, the tunnels and chambers become a spaghetti-like maze—perfect for confusing enemy ants and keeping the colony safe.

Ant species use chambers in different ways. Honey ants have swollen, honey-filled abdomens and hang from high-chamber ceilings. Harvester ants store seeds in shallow chambers. Leaf-cutter ants turn chambers into fungus gardens. Some ants keep aphids in special chambers and drink the sweet honeydew they produce.

Some nests, like those built by army ants, are only meant to last a short time. Others can last for decades or longer. Not all nests are built in soil. *Pseudomyrmex* make their nest in the hollow thorns of acacia trees. Weaver ants make nests out of leaves. The workers pull the leaves together and then use their larvae, which produce a sticky substance, to glue the leaves together! Nests may be built in the open with soldiers to guard the entrance or have hidden entrances under rocks or logs for protection. Sometimes ant colonies unite to form a supercolony made of thousands of interconnected nests that spread to other continents!

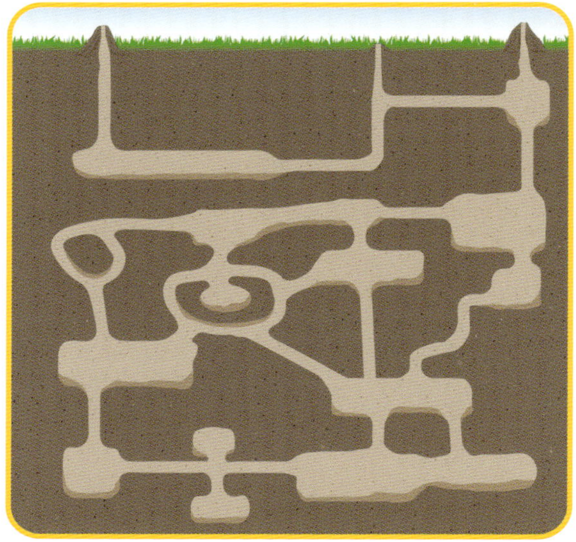

Worker ants dig smooth tunnels between the chambers of a nest.

Weaver ants use silk spun by their larvae to weave leaves into a nest.

Honeypot ants

A CLOSER LOOK

An ant nest may have more than just ants living in it. Nests are warm from all the ant activity and there is always lots of food around. This makes them attractive homes for other **arthropods**. Arthropods that live in ant nests are called guests or **myrmecophiles**. Some guests look just like the ants, so the colony thinks they are members. Some ants care for the guests like their own young. Others may not be welcome, but they are too slippery to catch, so they are allowed to stay. Some guests eat ant eggs and larvae. Scavenger guests eat dead and diseased ants. Scientists estimate there are more than 3,000 species of myrmecophiles, which include beetles, silverfish, mites, and roly-polies.

Communication

In their dark underground world, ants mostly communicate with odors, called **pheromones**. Ants can talk with pheromones like we talk with words. The "words" are made of mixtures of pheromones produced by glands in ants' bodies. One gland can produce an alarm scent and another may call for help. Yet another mixture may confuse enemies or send them away from the nest.

Touch is another method of ant communication. As the ants scurry through the dark tunnels of their nest, they touch each other with their antennae to check for their family's familiar scent. Workers ask for food from other workers by tapping their mouths. Even ant larvae communicate. They rock back and forth, demanding to be fed.

Ants also use sound and vibration to communicate. Most ants have a rough place on their abdomen that they rub to make high-pitched, squeaky sounds. Ants that get accidentally buried in a cave-in will squeak for help. Their nestmates feel in their legs the vibration caused by the squeaking and scurry to their rescue.

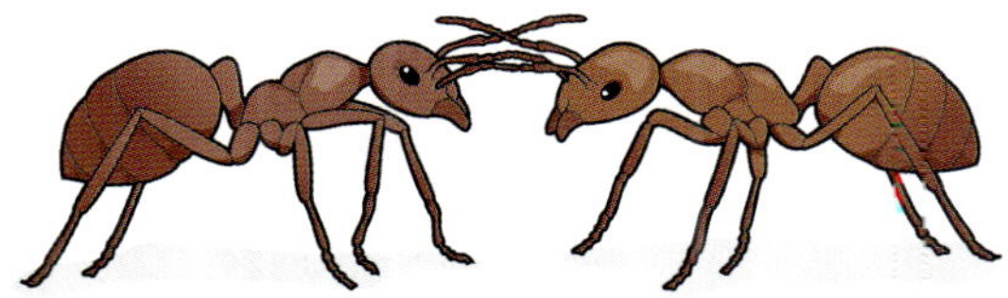

Ants use their sensitive antennae to check for their family's scent.

DID YOU KNOW?
Some anthills can be used as a compass. Ants build their hills so the longest slope is always facing south to soak up the sun's warmth.

JUNIOR SCIENTISTS IN ACTION

When ants have someplace to go, they will do what they can to stay on the trail. What happens if they run into a small obstacle? Ants are strong and can clear things like small pebbles or sticks off their trails to make it easier to carry food back to the nest. Will the ants in your neighborhood go around, climb over, or move an obstacle?

You will need:

- **AN ANT TRAIL**
- **GRAINS OF SAND**
- **SPRIGS OF GRASS**

1. Find some foraging ants and sprinkle a few sand grains in their path. Then, farther up the ant trail, place a few sprigs of grass. In another section of the trail, sprinkle a wide band of sand and grass, blocking the trail.
2. After 24 hours, check to see if the ants overcame the obstacles.

Finding Food

When it's time to eat, ants have different diets and different ways of getting food. Some meals are as close as the next ant! Ants are social and share food with their nestmates. They store a liquid in a body pouch called a crop. When an ant taps a nestmate's mouth with its leg, the ant spits out a tasty droplet. This behavior is called **trophallaxis**. It's not always just a snack. The liquid contains information about the ant and clues about the health and diet of the colony.

Ants eat many different kinds of food. Some ants are vegetarians and gather seeds on the ground or even pick their own. They chew off the husks and take the kernels back to their nests. Damp seeds are dried in the sun to prevent mold, then stored in chambers called granaries. Some ants feed on sweet sap from wounded plants. Leafcutter ants gather leaves to grow fungus for food.

Ants can pass food to each other by touching mouths, which looks like a kiss.

One species of ant doesn't hunt its own food. It steals it! These ants build their nests near other ant nests, then rob the worker ants returning with food. Other ant species act like dumpster divers and search through neighboring ants' kitchen trash! Army ants travel in large groups and visit other ant nests to steal their favorite foods—larvae and pupae. If food is scarce, some ants will eat their own babies to survive.

Some ant species hunt alone, each bringing food back to the nest. Other species work in groups. They use scout ants to locate food and get workers to help retrieve it. Scouts drag their abdomens on the ground and leave an odor trail to mark the way to the food. This trail also helps the foraging workers find their way back to the nest. Some odor trails can last for months and are called trunk trails because they look like a tree with branches, limbs, and twigs.

Ant trails are kept neat by workers who clear away small stones, sticks, and other debris. Hundreds of thousands of ants may use these trails every day. Some trails are so worn they are used by animals and even people. Ants can forage, or look for food, far from their nests. They are able to remember landmarks and use stars to help find their way back to the nest.

If you follow a line of ants, you'll likely find something they like to eat at the end of it!

DID YOU KNOW?

Adetomyrma venatrix, also known as the Dracula ant, lives in Madagascar. These ants are blind and have a bizarre habit. They drink the hemolymph, or "blood," of their larvae!

JUNIOR SCIENTISTS IN ACTION

You've learned that ants lay pheromone odor trails to guide their nestmates to a source of food or to a new nest site. Find out what happens when you break an odor trail!

You will need:

AN ANT TRAIL

SOAPY WATER

1. Locate ants that are walking in a line outside. They may be on a sidewalk or they could be following a board on a porch or deck. They might even be following a garden hose!
2. Dip your finger in the soapy water and rub a small section of the trail.
3. Observe what happens when the ants come to this spot in the trail. Do they cross it? Do they change directions? Do they abandon the trail?

Predators and Parasites

There is danger around every corner for ants. They are on the menu for many lizards, birds, and other insects. Ants can defend themselves by biting and stinging. Most female ants have a stinger connected to a poison gland. Some ant stings are super painful and can cause allergic reactions. Certain species spray poison instead of stinging to inject it.

Some insects have found ways around ants' defense mechanisms. Rove beetles lurk inside the ants' dark tunnels or wait near the nest entrance to ambush and kill returning workers. If they are attacked, the beetles spray a stinky odor, then run away. The antlion larva, also called a doodlebug, builds a cone-shaped pit trap in the sand. It buries itself at the bottom of the pit with its jaws open and waits. Ants that fall

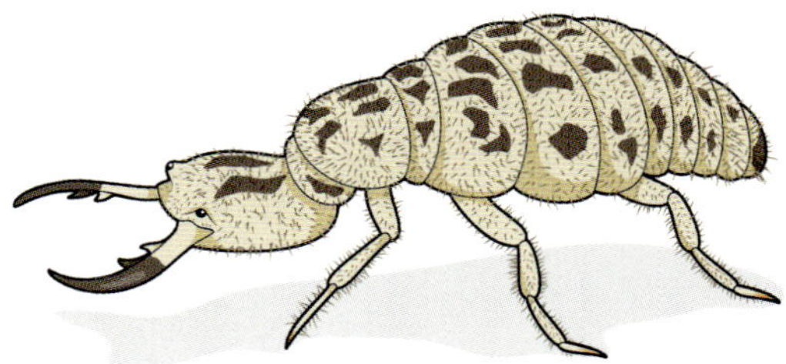

Rove beetles (top) and doodlebugs (bottom) are two predators that ants need to watch out for.

into the pit can't get out and slide right into the antlion's mouth!

Ants can also be attacked from the inside. **Parasites** develop inside an ant's body. One parasite, the phorid fly, lays its egg on an ant's head. The egg hatches into a tiny maggot that crawls into the ant's head to feed. The maggot pupates and when it becomes an adult, it pops out of the ant—making its head fall off! When ants hear these flies buzzing around, they panic. No wonder why!

DID YOU KNOW?

In 1983, Dr. Justin Schmidt developed the Schmidt sting pain index. This scale rates the stings of bees, ants, and wasps into four levels, according to how much they hurt. Level 4 pain is caused by bullet ants and tarantula hawk wasps. It is described as like being "trapped in the flow of an active volcano!"

Ant nest beetles feed on ant eggs, larvae, and even adult ants

A CLOSER LOOK

In some tropical regions of the world, ants occasionally begin to act very strange—like zombies! These ants are infected by a type of fungus that releases a chemical that controls the ant's behavior. "Zombie ants" will suddenly have the urge to climb a plant to a particular place where the light and moisture are just right. Exactly at noon, the ant crawls to the underside of a leaf and clamps onto the leaf with its mandibles. It uses incredible force, called a "death grip." Soon a fungus grows, gluing the ant to the leaf. When night falls, spores burst from the fungus and drift down to the forest floor. Other ants soon come into contact with the spores and get infected, too . . . creating more zombie ants!

Ant vs. Ant

Ants sometimes get into fights—for food and territory. Some species have special soldier workers with huge heads and jaws for fighting. Others use pheromones to alert the nest or confuse the enemy. Some ants capture other ants—not for food, but to use as slaves. To do this, some honeypot ant species attack weaker honeypot colonies. They kill the queen, capture workers, and then return to their own nests with their new servants.

Amazon ants have jaws shaped like knives that are perfect for killing other ants, but the jaws make it impossible to feed themselves, care for their young, or build a nest. These ants also need servants. When an Amazon ant scout returns with news of a nearby colony, the ants follow the odor trail to their victims' nest. Once there, they kill every worker they see and steal

An Argentine ant fighting a much larger fire ant.

Amazon ant

the pupae. When the adults emerge from the pupae, they get to work feeding and caring for their helpless Amazon captors.

Some ants trick their enemies. The tiny desert species *Conomyrma* has figured out how to trap their honeypot ant enemies. They drop tiny pebbles to plug the honeypot ant nest entrance, then safely hunt in the area without being attacked!

DID YOU KNOW?

People eat ants in many parts of the world. They are said to have a tangy, citrus flavor. In the countries Thailand and Laos in Southeast Asia, a weaver ant salad is made of weaver ant eggs, mint leaves, spring onion, chili, and fish sauce. This delicacy is even more expensive than meat!

Australian worker ant

JUNIOR SCIENTISTS IN ACTION

What foods do the ants in your neighborhood prefer? Sometimes a colony needs a quick source of energy, and a sugary food is at the top of their menu. Other times the ants go for proteins, like a dead insect or small piece of meat. Set up an ant buffet to see what they are craving.

You will need:

- AN ANT TRAIL OR ACTIVE NEST
- 4 SHALLOW DISHES (JAR LIDS WORK WELL, TOO)
- LOLLIPOP OR OTHER CANDY (WET THE LOLLIPOP FIRST)
- SMALL PIECE OF LUNCH MEAT OR HAMBURGER
- LEMON SLICE
- PIECE OF BREAD OR CRACKER

1. Look for an ant trail or ant nest that has active ants outside.
2. Put one type of snack in each dish.
3. Place the dishes near the ants and watch what happens.

How do the ants react? Which food did they first select? Leave the dishes out for a few hours and check back. Which dishes have the most ants?

Ants and Honeydew

Did you know that ants get food from other insects and protect them in return? This type of relationship is called **symbiotic**. Both the ants and the other insects are helped by their partnership. Tiny insects called aphids feed on plant sap and then ooze a sugary liquid from their butts that's called honeydew. Ants love the honeydew!

Ants tend large herds of aphids on plants to get honeydew. The ants build their nest at the base of the plant so they can protect their herds from harm. If the plant is disturbed, the ants rush out of their nest and up the stem to attack predators or tiny wasps trying to lay eggs in the aphids. The ants stroke the aphids with their antennae. In return, the aphids produce drops of delicious honeydew.

Caterpillars from a family of butterflies called Lycaenidae also make a

A field ant caring for aphids

A field ant caring for a caterpillar

sweet liquid that ants like. It seeps from pores on their bodies when ants stroke them. In return for the snack, ants defend the caterpillars from parasitic wasps and flies that try to lay eggs in them. Adult butterflies hunt for plants with ants because they know the ants will protect their young when they hatch.

DID YOU KNOW?
More than 200 species of birds use ants to rid themselves of external parasites, such as lice. The birds lie down on or near an anthill and stretch out their wings. Then they let the ants crawl on them. The birds prefer species of ants that spray **formic acid** rather than the ones that sting.

Ants tending to mealybugs

Ants and the Environment

Ants may be small, but they have a big impact on Earth. Ants dig nests and are constantly repairing and expanding them. Scientists believe they are as important as earthworms in moving and aerating soil! Ants are **decomposers**. Carpenter ants break apart fallen logs and stumps as they build their nests inside. Ants are also harvesters. Some species gather and spread seeds, which often sprout to create new plants.

Ants help people, too! Some species eat crop pests such as bollworms. They also feed on small, disease-carrying arthropods like ticks that carry Lyme disease. Ants are a favorite food for some birds and animals. If all the ants on Earth were to die, it would be catastrophic. We might see an increase in diseases, crop pests, and the extinction of insects and animals that depend on ants for food!

Some plants need ants to spread their seeds in order to survive.

DID YOU KNOW?

Young men of the Amazon Mawé tribe perform an unusual ritual to become warriors. Bullet ants are woven into a glove with their stingers pointing inside. The boys must wear the glove for 5 minutes—repeated 20 times over 1 month. The pain is so severe it numbs their arms each time!

Army Ants

Let's meet a group of ants that are different in many ways from all the others—army ants. There are more than 200 species of army ant, and they all have two things in common. They are fierce raiders that travel together and attack prey in large groups, and they build temporary nests. Army ants are found in the tropics. Their colonies can have 15 million members. They must constantly move to hunt food for their hungry army. Colonies grow so large that they split every three years. If the queen dies, the entire colony also dies unless they quickly join another colony.

Eciton burchelli army ants can be recognized by the "teeth" on the insides of their mandibles.

BUILT TO TRAVEL

Army ants are almost always on the move. They explore new territories by moving their nests from place to place in groups. Army ants are built for this traveling lifestyle. The colony's queen is blind, wingless, and has an enormous abdomen. She can produce three to four million eggs every month! It would

Army ant queen

be difficult for her to travel this way, so when it's time to get moving, the queen's abdomen shrinks. This way, she can keep up with the rest of her colony.

Male army ants are large and have wings and eyes to find new queens to mate with. Workers of some species are blind while others may have some sight. Despite their poor vision, the ants are able to travel in a group using odor and touch to stay together.

ON THE MOVE

Army ants march through the rain forest in different ways. Some travel on the surface, looking like thick, black living ropes. But many army ants move in hidden trails protected by soil walls or beneath soil arches, which makes them nearly invisible.

Army ants can form a living bridge or chain to make their way across obstacles.

Army ants may travel as a narrow column of workers or as a swarm that can spread as wide as 25 feet in the front. All army ants alternate between staying put and traveling, depending on what the queen is doing. If she's laying eggs, the colony settles in one place for a couple of weeks. Instead of digging a nest, the colony makes a **bivouac**. A bivouac is a nest made of living ants. To make a bivouac, the ants latch together with their claws, surrounding the queen and brood. The bivouac is made in a protected space, like a hollow log or between the roots of large tropical trees. Some species form nests in the ground and spend months in one location. When the queen is finished laying eggs, the colony starts moving again.

DID YOU KNOW?
Army ants that are blind sometimes lose their colony's odor trail and begin to follow one another instead. They begin to spiral, moving in circles until they die! This strange behavior is called an ant mill.

SOLDIERS AND WORKERS

Army ant workers must find enough food to feed their tremendous colony. As workers capture food, they move to the back of the line and new workers move forward to continue the raid. Prey that is too large to move is cut into pieces. The workers lay down odor trails for the swarm to follow. Workers also have to carry the larvae. They have jaws that are specially shaped for this job.

Army ants carrying larvae

Army ant soldiers have one job: protecting the colony. They have giant heads and jaws. Soldiers move along the edge of the swarm and keep watch for danger. These ants' jaws are so oversized, they can't feed themselves and have to depend on their nestmates to feed them.

JUNIOR SCIENTISTS IN ACTION

Many ants like to eat sweet things. Can they tell the difference in sweetness between two choices? It's time to find out with this simple experiment!

You will need:

- 2 SMALL PLASTIC CONTAINERS
- SUGAR
- WATER
- BLUE FOOD COLORING
- RED FOOD COLORING
- PAPER TOWEL

1. Mix 1 teaspoon of sugar in ¼ cup of water in a small container. Add two drops of red food coloring. This will be the less sweet liquid.
2. Mix 2 teaspoons of sugar in ¼ cup of water. Add two drops of blue food coloring. This will be the sweeter liquid.
3. Tear two small corners from the paper towel.
4. Quickly dip one piece of paper towel in the red water, then put it on another paper towel to soak up excess liquid. Do the same with the blue water.
5. Place both tiny sections of wet paper towel next to a foraging ant trail and see what happens!

Do the ants like the less sweet paper (red) best or do they prefer the sweeter paper (blue)? Do the ants like both? Do the ants avoid the papers completely?

EATING HABITS

A colony of millions of ants needs a lot of food. Army ants work together as a single group to hunt. These fierce hunters are able to take down prey many times their size. Nothing in their path is safe. Some species eat only centipedes, while others feed on termites or other insects. Swarms of army ants have also killed animals like frogs and snakes many times larger than themselves.

Army ants will kill and eat other species of ants, like this *Eciton vagans* bringing a trap-jaw ant back to the nest.

DID YOU KNOW?

Scientists discovered a tiny beetle, *Nymphister kronaueri*, that attaches to an army ant's petiole with its mandibles. It pulls in its antennae and legs close to its body to camouflage itself. It even smells like the army ants!

MAKE YOUR OWN ANT FARM

Do you want to watch ants up close? Try building a **formicary**—an artificial ant nest!

These instructions explain how to make a simple formicary at home, but you could also buy one in a store or online. If you buy one, make sure there is a manual or webpage explaining how to care for it and that you can take it apart to clean it. There also needs to be a way to add just the right amount of water. Before you begin making your own, you must decide if you are willing to take care of your colony. All pets require care and attention, including ants.

You will use this farm to observe worker ants only, because there will be no queen.

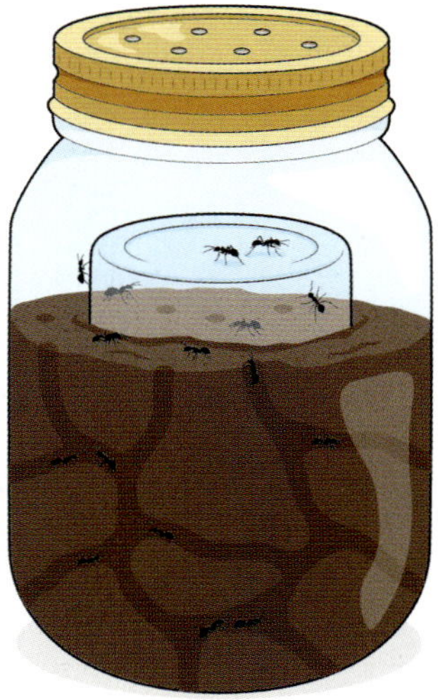

You will be able to watch them build their nest and feed but you won't see eggs and young ants. This ant farm will last a few weeks to a couple of months. If you grow tired of your pets, return the ants to the place where you found them.

You will need:

- ACTIVE ANT HILL
- SOIL FROM NEAR ANT HILL
- SPRAY BOTTLE FILLED WITH WATER
- 1 LARGE-MOUTHED SMOOTH JAR WITH LID
- 1 SMALLER JAR WITH LID (THE SMALL JAR NEEDS TO FIT INSIDE THE LARGE JAR COMPLETELY WITH ROOM OUTSIDE IT)
- SPOON
- COTTON SWAB
- OLIVE OIL
- SMALL NAIL
- HAMMER
- SMALL PIECE OF SWEET FOOD

Make Your Formicary

1. Locate an active ant hill.
2. Collect soil from near the ant-hill and place it in a box.
3. Lightly moisten the soil using a spray bottle and mix the soil until evenly moist. Adding the wrong amount of water is the number one reason ant colonies fail. Soil that is too wet can drown ants and cause mold to grow, which will quickly kill a colony.
4. Place the lid on the smaller jar and insert it inside the larger jar.

CONTINUED

MAKE YOUR OWN ANT FARM *CONTINUED*

5. Hold the small jar in the center of the large jar and carefully spoon the soil into the space between the two jars. Leave about 1 inch of space at the top of the large jar.
6. Lightly tap the jars on the table to compact the soil.
7. Use a cotton swab dipped in olive oil to wipe the inside of the large jar rim. This will prevent your ants from escaping.
8. Ask an adult to help you punch tiny air holes in the large lid. Make sure they are small enough that the ants can't escape.

Collect Your Ants

1. Set out a small piece of sweet food next to the anthill and leave it there for a few hours.
2. Return to the anthill and collect 12 to 25 ants. Use the spoon to pick up the food and ants.
3. Carefully place the ants in the ant farm.
4. Quickly screw on the large lid. Your ant farm is ready to observe!

Care for Your Ants

Ants are very easy to keep. Three times a week, or every other day, open the jar and use an eyedropper to add a few drops of

water to the soil. Stop adding water if you see condensation on the inside of the jar. Drop in a few grains of sugar every couple of days or small crumbs of cookie. Because there are no larvae, your ants will not need much protein, but you can add a small dead insect every two weeks for variety. If the ants don't eat it, remove the insect and discontinue feeding the ants other insects.

Observe and Learn

Once your ant farm is doing well, you can use it to try some experiments with your ants! These are just a couple of suggestions. Can you think of others?

ANT RACE

Do your ants have a favorite food? Let's find out! Place a small piece of sugary food in your formicary and use a timer to see how long it takes for them to find it. Write down the time. The next day, place a tiny piece of meat in your formicary and start your timer. Write down the new food-discovery time. Were the ants' food-finding times similar?

DAY OR NIGHT SHIFT?

Do your ants work during the day, during the night, or both? You can see for yourself. Make observations throughout the day to see if they are active in the morning and afternoon. After it gets dark, use a soft light to look at the colony and check to see if your ants are moving.

PART TWO

ANTS UP CLOSE

Now that you've learned a few things about our tiny neighbors, you probably would like to meet some. Read on to get acquainted with some ant species from all around the world. Which is your favorite?

Acrobat Ant

Crematogaster ashmeadi

SAY IT! *KREE-meh-toh-GAS-ter ash-MEE-dee*

There are about 400 species of acrobat ants in the world. They all have heart-shaped gasters. If it feels threatened, an acrobat ant can point its gaster up over its head—like a human acrobat. These ants like to nest in damp wood. Some take over beetle nests inside trees. Acrobat ants may also build a paper-like nest called a carton nest. They make the nest by chewing plants and mixing the goo with animal poop and soil. Some species like the Peruvian acrobat ant create tropical gardens by planting seeds in their carton nests. The plants camouflage the nest and the roots make it strong.

ANT FACTS

COMMON NAME: Acrobat ant	**SIZE:** .06 to .1 inch
SCIENTIFIC NAME: *Crematogaster ashmeadi*	**DIET:** Omnivorous; mostly honeydew, some dead insects
WHERE THEY'RE FOUND: Southern and eastern United States	**SIZE OF COLONY:** Medium to large

Argentine Ant

Linepithema humile

SAY IT! *line-pih-THEE-mah yoo-MIL-ee*

Argentine ants are expert world travelers! They were originally from Argentina and Uruguay in South America. When humans traveled by ship to these areas, Argentine ants hitched a ride out. In less than 100 years, they have spread all over the globe! As a matter of fact, these ants form one of the largest supercolonies that stretch across continents. Argentine ants are very hard to control because there are several queens in a single colony. New queens don't fly off to start new colonies; instead, they create a new colony by branching off of the parent colony.

ANT FACTS

COMMON NAME: Argentine ant	**SIZE:** .06 to .1 inch
SCIENTIFIC NAME: *Linepithema humile*	**DIET:** Omnivorous; honeydew, nectar, insects
WHERE THEY'RE FOUND: Worldwide	**SIZE OF COLONY:** Supercolonies can have billions of ants

Black Carpenter Ant

Camponotus pennsylvanicus

SAY IT! *kamp-oh-NOH-tus pen-sil-VAN-ih-kus*

If you see large dark ants scurrying in your house, chances are they are carpenter ants. These ants nest in wood. Sometimes they make their nests in wood found in human homes, especially if it is damp! These are large ants and they can make noise when they are chewing wood. You may be able to hear them chewing if you listen closely. Carpenter ants don't sting, but they can bite and squirt formic acid from their butts.

ANT FACTS

COMMON NAME: Black carpenter ant

SCIENTIFIC NAME: *Camponotus pennsylvanicus*

WHERE THEY'RE FOUND: Bermuda, Canada, United States

SIZE: .25 to .5 inch

DIET: Honeydew, fruit juices, plant sap, living and dead insects

SIZE OF COLONY: 2,000 to 15,000

Bullet Ant

Paraponera clavata

SAY IT! *pehr-ah-poh-NEHR-ah KLA-vah-tah*

Bullet ants are some of the largest ants in the world. They are about one inch long—almost as long as a paperclip. They are aggressive, which means they will attack at the slightest threat. Their sting is very painful. Some people say that being stung by a bullet ant hurts as much as being shot! That's where they get their name. These ants mostly live at the base of trees and forage the leaves at the top. Bullet ants are only found in the tropical regions of Central and South America.

ANT FACTS

COMMON NAME: Bullet ant	**SIZE:** .7 to 1.2 inches
SCIENTIFIC NAME: *Paraponera clavata*	**DIET:** Omnivorous; nectar, small insects, tree sap
WHERE THEY'RE FOUND: Central and South America	**SIZE OF COLONY:** 150,000 to 700,000

Eciton Army Ant

Eciton burchellii

SAY IT! *EH-sih-ton bur-CHEH-lee-eye*

Eciton army ants are called "swarm raiders." Their swarm fans out to form a "carpet" of ferocious workers, which can be more than 10 feet across and up to 650 feet long. That's more than twice as long as a football field! They kill every insect in their path and sometimes small animals like snakes, lizards, and some birds. To help their nestmates move more quickly while foraging, some workers settle into holes and crevices in the ground to create a smooth surface.

ANT FACTS

COMMON NAME: Eciton army ant

SCIENTIFIC NAME: *Eciton burchellii*

WHERE THEY'RE FOUND: Central and South America, Mexico, and Trinidad and Tobago

SIZE: .12 to .5 inch

DIET: Carnivorous; small insects, vertebrates like lizards and birds

SIZE OF COLONY: 100,000 to 2,000,000

Gigantiops

Gigantiops destructor

SAY IT! *JYE-gan-tee-ops deh-STRUK-tor*

What big eyes Gigantiops ants have—the largest of any ant in the world! Gigantiops have excellent vision and are especially attracted to movement. They hunt alone and have an unusual way of capturing their prey: They jump! These ants are shy and do not have a stinger. Sometimes Gigantiops will build their nest next to a bullet ant nest. Predators know to stay away from the ferocious bullet ants, so Gigantiops does not have to worry about them.

ANT FACTS

COMMON NAME: Gigantiops	**SIZE:** .4 to .6 inch
SCIENTIFIC NAME: *Gigantiops destructor*	**DIET:** Omnivorous; nectar, small insects
WHERE THEY'RE FOUND: South America	**SIZE OF COLONY:** Up to several hundred workers

Honey Ant

Myrmecocystus mexicanus

SAY IT! *mer-meh-koh-SIS-tus meks-ih-KAN-us*

Honey ants live in hot, dry places like deserts. Most species collect nectar from yucca plants. Storing food is important in places like deserts where food is scarce. But how do these ants safely store nectar? They use some of their nestmates as storage vessels! Special workers, called **repletes**, hang from the nest's ceiling. Other workers bring nectar back to the nest and give it to the repletes. The repletes' abdomens swell with nectar until they are as big as small grapes. When the colony is short on food, they eat the nectar from their living honey pots.

ANT FACTS

COMMON NAME: Honey ant	**SIZE:** .1 to .25 inch
SCIENTIFIC NAME: *Myrmecocystus mexicanus*	**DIET:** Omnivorous; aphids, sap, nectar, dead insects
WHERE THEY'RE FOUND: Mexico, United States	**SIZE OF COLONY:** About 5,000

Jack Jumper Ant

Myrmecia pilosula

SAY IT! *mer-MESH-ee-ah pye-loh-SOO-lah*

Jack jumper ants of Tasmania and Southeast Australia are large and one of the few ant species that are dangerous to humans. They are about a half inch long and attack their enemies with stingers *and* large jaws. Many people have a serious allergic reaction after being stung. Like other members of the genus *Myrmecia,* they are able to jump. This jumping ability and their good eyesight help them capture their insect prey. They are even fast enough to catch flies!

ANT FACTS

COMMON NAME: Jack jumper ant	**SIZE:** .5 inch
SCIENTIFIC NAME: *Myrmecia pilosula*	**DIET:** Carnivorous; small insects
WHERE THEY'RE FOUND: Australia	**SIZE OF COLONY:** 4,000 or more

Leafcutter Ant

Atta cephalotes

SAY IT! *AT-ah sef-ah-LOH-tees*

Leafcutter ants are fantastic fungus farmers! They have to be. It is the only thing they eat! These ants climb trees, cut leaves to just the right size to carry, and bring them back to the nest to put in their garden. They don't just grow and eat any fungus. It is a specific fungus related to parasol mushrooms. The fungus is normally handed down through generations in the colony. But sometimes a garden dies. When this happens, the only ways to get fungus to start a new garden are to join another colony or to steal some from a neighboring colony. Without the fungus, the colony will die.

ANT FACTS

COMMON NAME: Leafcutter ant

SCIENTIFIC NAME: *Atta cephalotes*

WHERE THEY'RE FOUND: Caribbean, Central and South America, Mexico

SIZE: .3 to .5 inch

DIET: Herbivorous; fungus

SIZE OF COLONY: Up to 5 million

Pavement Ant

Tetramorium immigrans

SAY IT! *teh-trah-MOH-ree-um IH-mih-grans*

Just as their name suggests, pavement ants often make their nests beneath pavement. They can also be found in houses where they have built their colony below the foundation. They are very common in the United States. If you spot tiny ants busily tending anthills between bricks or in the sidewalk, they are probably pavement ants. These little ants don't have large territories, but they fight to the death for the area around their colonies. Every spring, colonies of pavement ants face off and battle for space, often leaving thousands of dead by the time the war is over.

ANT FACTS

COMMON NAME: Pavement ant

SCIENTIFIC NAME: *Tetramorium immigrans*

WHERE THEY'RE FOUND: Argentina, Chile, North America

SIZE: About .1 inch

DIET: Omnivorous; small insects, seeds, nectar, pollen, dead animals, sweet human food

SIZE OF COLONY: About 10,000

Pharaoh Ant

Monomorium pharaonis

SAY IT! *mon-oh-MOH-ree-um FAIR-oh-nees*

Pharaoh ants are one of the world's most notorious insect pests. They live in the walls and foundations of millions of buildings in Europe and North America. These tiny ants are especially a problem in hospitals and nursing homes because they can transmit disease. Pharaoh ants are not picky eaters. Some have been found feeding on used bandages and shoe polish! The queens live only about three months—the shortest known life span of any ant queen. The colony produces multiple queens that can simply walk away with a few workers to create new colonies close by.

ANT FACTS

COMMON NAME: Pharaoh ant

SCIENTIFIC NAME: *Monomorium pharaonis*

WHERE THEY'RE FOUND: Worldwide

SIZE: .1 inch

DIET: Omnivorous; dead insects, seeds, nectar, fungus, sugary things

SIZE OF COLONY: 800 to 2,500

Red Imported Fire Ant

Solenopsis invicta

SAY IT! *soh-leh-NOP-sis in-VIK-tah*

Originally from Southern Brazil and Argentina, these fire ants are now found in many countries around the world. Red imported fire ants destroy crops and aggressively defend their nests. Their sting is painful and can cause small blisters. These ants know how to stick together! If they are threatened by flooding, they make a raft by linking together. The queen and young are protected in the center. They continue to float until the water dries up.

ANT FACTS

COMMON NAME: Red imported fire ant

SCIENTIFIC NAME: *Solenopsis invicta*

WHERE THEY'RE FOUND: Australia, Caribbean, China, Mexico, South America, United States

SIZE: .1 to .24 inch

DIET: Carnivorous; insects, spiders, earthworms

SIZE OF COLONY: Up to 250,000 workers

Trap-Jaw Ant

Odontomachus bauri

SAY IT! *oh-DON-toh-MAH-shoos BOH-ree*

Blink and you'll miss the trap-jaw ant's amazing hunting technique. These ants have strong jaws that can close extremely fast—much faster than the blink of an eye. This ant holds its jaws open as it patrols for prey. A long sensitive hair sticks out from its jaws. If the hair touches anything, the jaws snap closed—usually trapping a meal. The jaws close so forcefully that the action can propel the ant backward. This is helpful when trying to escape an enemy!

ANT FACTS

COMMON NAME: Trap-jaw ant	**SIZE:** .5 inch
SCIENTIFIC NAME: *Odontomachus bauri*	**DIET:** Carnivorous; insects and sometimes sweets
WHERE THEY'RE FOUND: Galapagos, Mexico, South America, Trinidad and Tobago	**SIZE OF COLONY:** Fewer than 200

Turtle Ant

Cephalotes varians

SAY IT! *sef-ah-LOH-tees VAIR-ee-ans*

Many ants make nests in the ground, but the turtle ant lives in hollowed parts of mangrove trees and hollow standing grass. Some workers in the colony have flat heads that look like dishes. They use their heads as plugs to cover the nest entrances and to push intruders out. Their heads are good for something else—as parachutes when the ants are falling to the ground from high branches. Turtle ants are scavengers, which means they eat dead things they find—usually freshly killed insects.

ANT FACTS

COMMON NAME: Turtle ant

SCIENTIFIC NAME: *Cephalotes varians*

WHERE THEY'RE FOUND: Caribbean, United States

SIZE: .1 to .6 inch

DIET: Omnivorous; wide variety of insects and honeydew

SIZE OF COLONY: About 1,000

Weaver Ant

Oecophylla smaragdina

SAY IT! *oh-ee-KAH-fil-ah smuh-RAG-dee-nah*

Weaver ants live in treetops. These amazing ant architects build their nests out of leaves that they glue together with their larvae's help. The soldiers work together to pull leaves close together. Then the workers grab some larvae and get to work. The workers tap the larvae on their heads to get them to secrete silk threads that the workers use to "sew" the leaves together. Weaver ant nests can be large and stretch across several trees! These ants feed on honeydew from insects, including scale insects.

ANT FACTS

COMMON NAME: Weaver ant

SCIENTIFIC NAME: *Oecophylla smaragdina*

WHERE THEY'RE FOUND: Australia, India, Sri Lanka

SIZE: .2 to .4 inch

DIET: Omnivorous; insects and honeydew

SIZE OF COLONY: Up to 500,000

Western Thatching Ant

Formica obscuripes

SAY IT! *for-MY-kah ob-SKYOO-rih-pees*

Another incredible ant architect is the western thatching ant. This species builds huge anthills—sometimes six feet high—made entirely of plant material. They will use twigs, pine needles, grass stems, or whatever else is near the nest to build a large mound. The nest also extends as deep as four feet into the ground. The mound helps control the temperature inside. Thatching ants may have more than one queen and more than one interconnected nest. If disturbed, these ants become aggressive. They rush out of the nest and spray formic acid at the threat.

ANT FACTS

COMMON NAME: Western thatching ant

SCIENTIFIC NAME: *Formica obscuripes*

WHERE THEY'RE FOUND: United States, Western Canada

SIZE: .15 to .3 inch

DIET: Omnivorous; sap, nectar, seeds, carrion, birds, and small mammals

SIZE OF COLONY: About 40,000; some reports of 56 million in a supercolony

GLOSSARY

ARTHROPOD: Any animal with an exoskeleton, a body made of segments or parts, and jointed legs

BIVOUAC: The temporary nest of army ants, composed of living ants clinging together in a ball

COLONY: A group or community of a single species living together

COMPOUND EYE: A large eye made up of many small lenses

DECOMPOSER: An organism that eats dead plants or animals and turns them into nutrients for living plants

DRONE: A male insect with only one job—to mate with the queen

EUSOCIALITY: When a species has one female, only a few males for breeding, and many non-breeding workers that cooperate together to take care of the young and the colony as a whole

FORMIC ACID: An acid produced by ants that burns on contact

FORMICARY: An artificial ant nest to keep ants for observation or as pets

FOSSIL: A print, or parts of prehistoric plants or animals, left in stone

GASTER: The large bulb-like part of an ant's abdomen that holds the organs

INVERTEBRATE: An animal without a backbone—such as an insect, crustacean, or worm

MIDDEN: An ant trash pile

MYRMECOPHILE: An organism that lives with ants in their nest

MYRMECOLOGIST: A scientist who studies ants

OCELLI: Small simple eyes that can detect light, but can't see images

OMNIVORE: An animal that eats both plants and other animals

PARASITE: An organism that lives on or inside another and takes nutrients from it

PETIOLE: An ant's waist that is so narrow that only liquid food can pass through it into the abdomen

PHEROMONE: A chemical that an animal makes to communicate with other animals, usually of the same species

PUPA/PUPAE: The sleeping stage of an insect when they are inside a silken cocoon or hardened exoskeleton

REPLETE: A worker ant that can store so much nectar in its abdomen or gaster that it swells

SPECIES: A group of living things that have many things in common and can mate to make others of their kind

SYMBIOTIC: The relationship between two different living things that helps one or both survive

TROPHALLAXIS: When an ant shares a liquid from their stomach with other ants and guests that live in their nest, called myrmecophiles

MORE TO EXPLORE

BOOKS

Dr. Eleanor's Book of Common Ants
by Eleanor Spicer Rice and Rob Dunn

The Life and Times of the Ant
by Charles Micucci

Our Amazing World: Ants
by Kay de Silva

Who Would Win: Green Ants vs. Army Ants by Jerry Pallotta

WEBSITES

Ant Maps
AntMaps.org

Ant Web
AntWeb.org

Ants Canada
AntsCanada.com

AntWiki
AntWiki.org

Aus Ants
AusAnts.net

INDEX

ACKNOWLEDGMENTS

The author wishes to acknowledge all the myrmecologists whose curiosity and dedication have led to great discoveries in ant biology and taxonomy. There are many famous myrmecologists, including William Morton Wheeler, Bert Hölldobler, Edward O. Wilson, and Barry Bolton, to name just a few. The author also wishes to thank Alex Wild, whose photographs bring the ants in this book "alive."

ABOUT THE AUTHOR

BEVERLY GERDEMAN, PhD, has been an entomologist since 2002, specializing in pest management. She has worked in Indonesia, the Philippines, sub-Saharan Africa, and Eastern Europe. She loves to chase army ants and hunt for rare myrmecophiles!